Make It HAPPEN!

Ashima Shiraishi

ROCK CLIMBER

BY DAN GUNDERMAN

Lightswitch
LEARNING

150 East 52nd Street, Suite 32002
New York, NY 10022
www.lightswitchlearning.com

Educators and Librarians, for a variety of teaching resources, visit www.lightswitchlearning.com

Library of Congress Cataloging-in-Publication Data is available upon request.
Library of Congress Catalog Card Number pending

ISBN: 978-1-68265-578-8
ISBN: 1-68265-578-4

Ashima Shiraishi by Dan Gunderman

Edited by Lauren Dupuis-Perez
Book design by Sara Radka
The text of this book is set in Neuton Regular.

Printed in China

Image Credits

Cover: Newscom, Xinhua/Liang Xu
Page 1: See credits for cover
Page 4: Getty Images, arabianEye RF
Page 5: (top) Alamy; (middle) Getty Images, Aurora Open; (bottom) Getty Images
Page 6: Alamy
Page 7: Getty Images
Page 8: Newscom, Erich Schlegel/ZUMAPRESS
Page 9: Getty Images, iStockphoto
Page 10: Getty Images, Aurora Open
Page 11: Getty Images, iStockphoto
Page 12: Newscom, Erich Schlegel/ZUMAPRESS
Page 13: Getty Images

Page 14: Getty Images; iStockphoto
Page 15: Getty Images, Blend Images
Page 16: Newscom
Page 17: Getty Images, Hero Images
Page 18: Getty Images
Page 19: Getty Images
Page 20: Newscom, Erich Schlegel/ZUMAPRESS
Page 22: Newscom, Xinhua/Liang Xu
Page 23: Newscom, Xinhua/Liang Xu
Page 24: Getty Images
Page 25: Getty Images, iStockphoto

"The challenge is to get
back up after each fall."

ASHIMA SHIRAISHI

•   •   •

Make It! HAPPEN!

Before Reading

Think about your own goals. Do you want to play soccer or write stories or make music? All of these activities take time and practice.

During Reading

During reading, keep an eye out for the highlighted vocab words. While learning about Ashima's story, pay attention to how she got to where she is today. What **skills** has she shown that have helped her **career**? In each chapter, the Make It Happen! activity will help you, too, build skills to reach your own goals.

After Reading

Look in the back of the book for questions and activities to help you think about Ashima's story. Share these with a friend, parent, or teacher. Also, talk about the skills you need to reach your goals.

skill: the ability to do something that comes from training, experience, or practice

career: a job that someone does for a long time

Contents

Early Life

Ashima first started rock climbing in Central Park.

One afternoon in New York City in 2007, Ashima Shiraishi was playing in Central Park. She saw a rock that many people were climbing. Even though she was just six years old, Ashima wanted to climb it too. The next day, she tried her first climb. She made it up a few feet, then fell. But Ashima had **initiative**. She came back the next day and kept trying until she succeeded.

Central Park is located in New York City.

Today, Ashima is a successful rock climber. She is a rising star in **bouldering** and **sport climbing**. She climbs outdoors and at climbing gyms. A climbing gym has climbing walls where people can practice indoors.

Ashima was born in New York City. Her parents are from Japan. Her father is Hisatoshi "Poppo" Shiraishi. He used to be a dancer. Her mother is Tsuya Otake. Tsuya sews Ashima's unique climbing pants.

initiative: the energy and desire to take action

bouldering: a type of rock climbing that is done without ropes or other safety equipment

sport climbing: a type of rock climbing that is done with straps and ropes

7

Ashima and one of her coaches, Obe Carrion, worked together for four years.

Life off the Rock

Ashima has always worked very hard at school. She pushes for straight As. Many times, that means staying up late. Ashima often does not get home from climbing until 8:30 p.m. In 2016, she moved to a new school for students who are already working on a **professional** career. In a YouTube video, Ashima said she was excited to go there because the new school would allow her to travel more. She would be able to go rock climbing more often. She was also excited to meet new friends. The other students there have strong **passions**, just like she does.

professional: relating to a job that requires special training, education, or skill

passion: something that you enjoy or love doing very much

Ashima likes climbing and works hard at it. She also makes time to see friends and do other things she enjoys. On a website called *The Players' Tribune* she wrote, "I love cooking, going to fashion shows, [and] shopping for shoes. When I'm with my friends, we don't really talk about climbing at all. We talk about what normal school kids talk about."

Make It! HAPPEN!

Create a Schedule

Ashima worked hard to become a rock climber. She practiced whenever she could. Do you have a favorite sport or special **talent**? Extra practice can help you improve your skills. Make your own practice plan that includes:

- when to wake up
- when to go to school
- when to practice your sport or talent
- when to spend time with family
- when to do homework

talent: a special ability that allows someone to do something well

Follow your schedule for a week. Were you able to stick to it? Does it need to be changed? Have you improved from the extra practice?

First Steps of the Journey

The sport of climbing is becoming more popular. It will be in the Olympic Games for the first time in 2020.

At first, Ashima didn't have the right shoes for rock climbing. Her tennis shoes made her slip and fall. Her family did not have extra money. But her parents knew she liked climbing, so they bought her climbing shoes. The new shoes helped Ashima climb better. They were small and light, with padding at the ankles and a rubber sole. Climbing shoes come in bright colors like red and yellow, and many have Velcro instead of shoelaces!

Rock climbers wear special shoes so that they do not slip.

route: a path by which a climber reaches the end of a climb

V Scale: a range of numbers that is used to show how hard a climb is

The first rock Ashima climbed in Central Park had many different **routes**. In bouldering, each route has a number and a fun name. The number tells athletes how hard it is to climb. Today, climbers use the **V Scale**. Routes that are V0-V2 are for beginners. Routes that are V9 and higher are only for very experienced climbers. Ashima's first route was a V0 called *Easy Overhang*.

Ashima's dad often helps spot Ashima. Spotters are there to keep climbers safe.

The Way to the Top

Only two years after she started climbing, Ashima won a big **competition**. At eight years old, she became the youngest person to climb a V10 boulder. By age 10, she became the youngest person to climb a V13.

When climbing, Ashima rubs **chalky** powder on her hands. This helps her hold on. She can use it at any time during a climb to help keep her hands from slipping off the rock. This chalk is also used in baseball and gymnastics.

competition: a contest where people try to win by being better or faster than others

chalk: a type of powder used by athletes to help them grip equipment or rocks

Climbers try different ways to move on the rocks. Ashima's dad, Poppo, helps her with this. Poppo tells her to look at a climb and then make a plan for her movements. "Even though he had never climbed, he was a professional dancer, and there are a lot of similarities between climbing and dancing," Ashima wrote for the website *The Players' Tribune*.

Make It! HAPPEN!

Make an Equipment List

Some sports need special equipment. For example, in baseball, you need a mitt, a helmet, a uniform, and cleats.

- Pick a new sport or activity you want to try.
- Make a list of equipment you need.
- Don't forget safety gear!
- Compare your list with your friends' or classmates' lists.

How are your lists similar? Did you forget anything?

Overcoming Obstacles

Climbers must be careful. A fall could cause them to get hurt.

Climbing takes a lot of work and time. But Ashima is still a typical kid. She has to balance school, friends, and her job as a climber. Now that Ashima is traveling more, finding a balance is even harder.

Professional rock climbers are usually in their 20s or 30s, and most are men. Ashima is young and small for a climber, so she had to **adapt** for her small size. She created a way to climb that fits her body. She uses her strength and **flexibility**. In *The Players' Tribune*, she wrote, "... [W]omen can be just as good as men. I've climbed [rocks] some grown men can't even do."

When climbing, athletes need to be able to balance using very small cracks and ledges.

adapt: to change something so it works better
flexibility: the ability to bend easily

Mt. Hiei is located outside of Kyoto, Japan. That's where Ashima climbed the V15 route *Horizon*.

Getting Back Up

Ashima also has to face difficult climbs. In December 2015, Ashima went to Japan to try a very hard route called *Horizon*. On her last day, she almost finished. But she fell. She tried a few more times, but kept slipping. Later that spring, she went back. "This time," she wrote in *The Players' Tribune*, "I didn't fall. [...] I was the first female and the youngest person ever to [climb] it."

Rock climbing can be dangerous. Ashima might get hurt doing what she loves. In 2016 at a climbing gym, she fell 45 feet. An ambulance took her to the hospital. But she only had a bruised back. She went home a few hours later. Ashima told NBC News, "I felt like that injury made me think about how **valuable** climbing is to my life. I think it made me grow as a climber, but it didn't make me scared of climbing or scared of falling."

valuable: very important or useful

Make It! HAPPEN!

Pick a Career

Knowing what type of career you want can help you plan for your future. Let's do some career planning now.

- Research careers you are interested in. Do you want to be a doctor? A professional soccer player? A teacher or an actor? Or something else?
- Pick one and make a list of skills you will need for the job.
- What things can you do to learn the skills you will need? Write them down.
- Give your plan to a fellow student or teacher.

What new skills can you start working on now to prepare for this career?

Teamwork

Some climbers work in teams. They must trust each other to reach the top.

Ashima reached the top of her sport in only a few years. Some people think she is the best climber today. Ashima has had the help of many people. Her family is very important. They travel with her, and Poppo is always there. He is her coach on the rock and a helpful support in her life.

When climbing, Ashima faces a lot of **pressure**, especially at competitions. She might fall. Or she might lose. Ashima has to keep up a strong "mental game." This means she has to **focus** on climbing and cannot think about things like school or friends. Poppo helps her do this. He always advises her to "have a quiet […] mind." A quiet mind helps Ashima with **problem-solving** during a difficult climb. That way, she can reach the top—and win.

A coach can help a climber improve in the sport.

pressure: a feeling of stress because people are depending on you for something

focus: to direct your attention or effort at something specific

problem-solving: the process or act of finding a solution to a problem

If Ashima falls, a spotter can help protect her head, neck, and back.

Support from All Sides

Poppo helps Ashima in each and every climb. Before Ashima begins, Poppo rubs lotion onto her forehead. He combs her hair. This helps her focus on the work ahead. Poppo also carries Ashima's things. He gets her pumped up and leads her in stretches.

Ashima's mother, Tsuya, helps her focus on her school work. Tsuya also makes Ashima's climbing pants. They are colorful, with bright yellow, purple, or lime-green designs. This gives Ashima a special look when she climbs.

Rock climbers support each other, too. How old you are or where you come from does not matter. Climbers want to **collaborate**. They want to make the sport better. Ashima is friends with the famous rock climber Dai Koyamada. Koyamada has become a **mentor** to Ashima. He encourages her to push herself and try new routes. Ashima was able to climb *Horizon* because of his help. Ashima now encourages other climbers to try *Horizon*.

collaborate: to work with another person or group in order to achieve or do something

mentor: someone who teaches or gives help and advice to a less experienced person

Make It! HAPPEN!

Build a Community

If you're interested in trying something new, building a community can help you. You can do this by starting a club. Club members can share ideas and give advice.

- Decide what your club will focus on.
- Write down goals for your club.
- Talk to your teacher about registering your club with your school.
- Find new members. Talk to people about your club and hand out fliers.
- Start holding meetings at least once a month.

How has this new community helped you reach your goals?

Current Career

Year after year, Ashima finishes more and more difficult climbs.

Ashima is now well known in the sports world. You can read about her in magazines. You can see her climb in online videos. Ashima continues to push herself. She has **perseverance** and takes every opportunity she is offered. Her parents, teachers, friends, and fellow climbers have helped her along the way. Because of this, she has been very successful.

Ashima gains more fans every year. In 2017, she reached 60,000 "likes" on Facebook.

perseverance: the quality that allows someone to continue trying to do something even though it is difficult

pacing: controlling or setting the speed

nerves: feelings of being worried or afraid

In 2016 and 2017, Ashima won many competitions. One of them was in March 2017 in Colorado. Ashima and only one other person finished the women's final climb. Ashima told NBC News, "As I was climbing, I had to focus on **pacing** myself [...] and focus on the climbing instead of falling down and not being able to control my **nerves**." She said when she reached the top, "I was so relieved and just happy. I couldn't really believe it."

Having slippery fingers can cause a climber to lose their grip on the rock.

The Power Struggle

Sometimes it only takes one minute to win it all. This was the case for Ashima in 2017 during an event called the Power Struggle. She finished a climbing wall in less than a minute. First, Ashima used her arms to pull herself up. Moving up the wall, she used her feet. During one move, her body hung from her fingertips, which were pressed into the pegs on the wall.

Ashima was almost there. She held on with only her right hand and right foot. Later, she was almost **parallel** with the ground. She used her strong arms and flexible legs to keep going. Finally, she had one move to go. She pulled back a little. She looked like she was about to leap like a frog. She quickly **extended** her body and grabbed on to the top!

The crowd cheered loudly. Ashima waved to her fans. Then, she dropped all the way down, landing on the mats on the ground. Victory!

parallel: lines, paths, etc., that are the same distance apart along their whole length and do not touch at any point

extend: to cause something, such as your arm or leg, to straighten or stretch out

Make It HAPPEN! Set Your Goals

Ashima has goals for her future. Some of them are things like doing harder climbs and going to the Olympics in 2020. Write and share your own goals.

• Write down three goals.
• Share them with three friends.
• Return to the list one year from now.
• Add new goals.

Did you reach your goals? Did writing down your goals help you achieve them?

Defining Moments

Ashima is still a teenager. But she has done a lot. She has already been tested by many rocks and competitions.

2007

Ashima completes her first bouldering route, *Easy Overhang*, at New York City's Central Park.

2012

At 10 years old, she climbs the *Crown of Aragorn*, a V13. It is located in Hueco Tanks, Texas. She becomes the youngest person to climb a rock that difficult.

2015

Ashima climbs her second V13-V14, a rock called *The Swarm*. She was the first female to do it. Also in 2015, she couldn't finish the V15 *Horizon* in Japan.

2015 & 2016

In 2015 and 2016, Ashima goes to the IFSC World Youth Championships. She wins in her group both times.

2016

Ashima has a scary 45-foot fall. She recovers quickly and comes back to compete just days later.

2016

Ashima returns to climb the V15 *Horizon* in Japan. This time, she succeeds.

2017

Ashima takes first place at the Power Struggle in Connecticut and the USA Climbing Sport & Speed Open National Championships in Colorado. Her next major goal is to reach the 2020 Olympics.

Depth of Knowledge

1 Explain how Ashima's 45-foot fall and going to the hospital affected her.

2 Describe how Ashima's parents help her achieve her goals.

3 Explain how Ashima's adaptability, initiative, and problem-solving skills make her a better rock climber.

4 Write an opinion piece on the future of rock climbing. What do you think rock climbing will be like in the future? How do you think Ashima is changing rock climbing? Use examples from this book.

5 If your friend said they wanted to go rock climbing for the first time, what would you tell them? Make a list of the most important things they would need to know. Then describe in detail how they can reach the top of a climbing-gym wall.

A Rock Climbing Adventure

In a small group, work together to design, draw, and label a large boulder to climb. Then write a plan for a rock climber to travel to the boulder and climb to the top.

MATERIALS NEEDED

- Poster board or large sheet of poster paper
- Markers in many different colors
- Pencils and paper

STEPS TO TAKE

1 Draw a large boulder. Label where a rock climber would start and where they would finish.

2 Make a travel plan for a rock climber to visit the boulder. How should they travel there? What do they need to pack? Use the Equipment List from page 13 for ideas.

3 Use different colored markers. Have each group member draw a climbing route from the start to the finish.

4 Have each member describe their path. Beyond physical fitness, what skills would they need? Review the Glossary on page 30 for examples.

5 Collaborate to turn your work into a short story. Write about how your rock climber prepared to climb your boulder. Did they follow a schedule to meet their goals? Review the schedule you wrote for the Make It Happen! activity on page 9. Write about how your climber traveled to your boulder. Describe what equipment they used and how they reached the top. What skills did the climber need to succeed?

Glossary

adapt *(verb)* to change something so it works better (pg. 15)

bouldering *(noun)* a type of rock climbing that is done without ropes or other safety equipment (pg. 7)

career *(noun)* a job that someone does for a long time (pg. 4)

chalk *(noun)* a type of powder used by athletes to help them grip equipment or rocks (pg. 12)

collaborate *(verb)* to work with another person or group in order to achieve or do something (pg. 21)

competition *(noun)* a contest where people try to win by being better or faster than others (pg. 12)

extend *(verb)* to cause something, such as your arm or leg, to straighten or stretch out (pg. 25)

flexibility *(noun)* the ability to bend easily (pg. 15)

focus *(verb)* to direct your attention or effort at something specific (pg. 19)

initiative *(noun)* the energy and desire to take action (pg. 7)

mentor *(noun)* someone who teaches or gives help and advice to a less experienced person (pg. 21)

nerves *(noun)* feelings of being worried or afraid (pg. 23)

pacing *(verb)* controlling or setting the speed (pg. 23)

parallel *(adjective)* lines, paths, etc., that are the same distance apart along their whole length and do not touch at any point (pg. 25)

passion *(noun)* something that you enjoy or love doing very much (pg. 8)

perseverance *(noun)* the quality that allows someone to continue trying to do something even though it is difficult (pg. 23)

pressure *(noun)* a feeling of stress because people are depending on you for something (pg. 19)

problem-solving *(verb)* the process or act of finding a solution (pg. 19)

professional *(noun)* relating to a job that requires special training, education, or skill (pg. 8)

route *(noun)* a path by which a climber reaches the end of a climb (pg. 11)

skill *(noun)* the ability to do something that comes from training, experience, or practice (pg. 4)

sport climbing *(noun)* a type of rock climbing that is done with straps and ropes (pg. 7)

talent *(noun)* a special ability that allows someone to do something well (pg. 9)

valuable *(adjective)* very important or useful (pg. 17)

V Scale *(noun)* a range of numbers that is used to show how hard a climb is (pg. 11)

Read More

Guillain, Charlotte. *Extreme Athletes: True Stories of Amazing Sporting Adventurers.* Chicago, Ill.: Raintree, 2014.

Ignotofsky, Rachel. *Women in Sports: 50 Fearless Athletes Who Played to Win.* New York: Ten Speed Press, 2017.

Romero, Jordan and Linda LeBlanc. *No Summit out of Sight: The True Story of the Youngest Person to Climb the Seven Summits.* New York: Simon & Schuster Books for Young Readers, 2014.

Stabler, David. *Kid Athletes: True Tales of Childhood from Sports Legends.* Philadelphia, Penn.: Quirk Books, 2015.

Zuckerman, Gregory. *Rising Above: How 11 Athletes Overcame Challenges in Their Youth to Become Stars.* New York: Philomel Books, 2016.

Internet Links

https://www.sikids.com/si-kids/2015/11/30/sportskid-year-2015-meet-finalists

http://choices.scholastic.com/story/should-teens-do-extreme-sports

https://www.youtube.com/watch?v=kc2f1gGLdHM

https://vimeo.com/55184231

http://www.tedxteen.com/talks/just-climb-through-it-ashima-shiraishi

Bibliography

Lowell, Josh and Peter Mortimer. *Reel Rock 11.* Big UP Productions, Sender Films, 2017. Web. 1 Apr. 2017.

The North Face. "Ashima Shiraishi: A Strong Mind." *YouTube.* YouTube, 30 Nov. 2016. Web. 14 June 2017.

Paumgarten, Nick. "The Most Talented Climber in the World?" *The New Yorker.* The New Yorker, 13 June 2017. Web. 14 June 2017.

Shiraishi, Ashima. "Just a Normal History-Making Rock-Climbing Teenage Girl." *The Players' Tribune.* The Players' Tribune, Inc., 09 Feb. 2017. Web. 14 June 2017.

Yap, Audrey Cleo. "15-Year-Old Ashima Shiraishi Nabs First Place at USA Climbing Championships." *NBCNews.com.* NBCUniversal News Group, 14 Mar. 2017. Web. 14 June 2017.

Index